I AM HALF FULL BUT THAT VOID IN ME IS A VOID
IN YOU; EVEN WHEN OUR FULLNESS PROPELS
US TO SPILL INTO ONE ANOTHER WE WILL
ALWAYS BE SOMEWHAT EMPTY.

-- ADRIAN MICHAEL

TITLES YOU MIGHT LIKE
BY
ADRIAN MICHAEL

--

loamexpressions

blinking cursor

notes of a denver native son

blackmagic

lovehues

notes from a gentle man

blooming hearts

Published by Creative Genius Publishing—
an imprint of A.Michael Ventures | Denver, CO

To contact the author visit adrianmichaelgreen.com
Cover art provided by Shutterstock.com

ISBN-13: 978-1522777212
ISBN-10: 1522777210

Printed in the United States of America

lovehues

what follows is an open letter dedicated to my heart.

i love
to feel
for
without
love
i'd lose
parts
of you—
parts
you gave me
to save me

i am
because
of you

i'm not looking
for a happy ending
but countless times
when we
stand in the fire
and burn
together

sky love
is the best love
it has no end
and even if
our temperature drops
and the winter changes
my love
is always there
in all
four seasons

i have wreaked havoc and left shrapnel shells
blazing hot and smoky in a past lifetime. there
was something liberating about your sky that
night: the atmosphere cascaded a green tinge, a
shade reminiscent of jazz and blues, melancholy
and joyous. somehow we collided, our
electrically charged particles danced with the
diamond asterisks and held them with stunning
gravity. redemptive in your ways, i was baptized
when you and i made impact.

y o u f l a s h e d y o u r s o u l a n d i h a v e
b e e n c h a s i n g y o u e v e r s i n c e.

forgive me but all my life my malnourished heart
has never tasted such light. i may never catch up to
you, a few steps behind, but keep me in sight so the
evaporated scent lingers on my lips.

your faults
are beauty marks
you wouldn't
be you
without them

you hold my soul tight when i just
want to fall apart.

days like this i can't
explain how i feel or
tell you what i need.

no matter how hard i try,
i'm flooded with emptiness.

perhaps the chaos inside of me escaped.

i need you when it returns.

i wish i could see
inside of your heart

your words
taste like honey
they drip
from your mouth
&
the fall of
sweet sound
is a wave
of arias
with a bouqet of
daffodils

in the heat of our moments
you are the cradle to my soul
and i love
that no matter
how scorching hot it gets
i know
you'd never leave my side

if you guard your soul from heartbreak,
you'll always be formidable.
don't be a stone wall.

let love in.

nothing
is more beautiful
than someone
with scars.

you and i
were written with no
beginning, no end.
our journey,
a simple middle passage,
is on us
to forge a path.

isn't that what perfection is?
imperfect people that balance our madness.

if i had two hearts
i'd give you one
to represent
my infinite love

don't fix me
just listen
i want
to be heard

i may fail to love you
the way you deserve
but each day i will try
because i know
if i lose you
i've lost it all

i wear you wherever i go
because i am a visual lover

lovekeeper
heartstealer
shipsinker
loveshaker
shipanchor
hearthealer

//you

back then i wouldn't
have been ready to
accept your love; i had
to destroy parts of myself
that wouldn't have served us.

you are the fire no one could contain.
you are your own master. that's the thing,
no one can control how a fire burns.
once you embrace that, you must nurture its
chaotic path. and your fire never dies, the smoke
becomes stars. you are the unstoppable element.

i don't care about your past
or who you were
i love who you are
and the future we're building now

what is a home without you in it?

and why is lonliness my darkest fear?

both leave me empty with worry

i need you near to subdue these thoughts

massage your love all over me

please be my shelter

i love you my dear

i needed someone who wasn't hell-bent
on fixing me. someone without an agenda.
someone who saw beauty marks instead of
flaws. someone who wouldn't leave me
when my past caught up with me. someone
who would love me. unconditionally.

//thank you

i don't want to show you off, or brag, not
even put you on display. i just want to pay
you back for saving me from my own
destruction by loving and serving
your every need.

i was way too nostalgic.
holding onto loose memories
as if they still existed.
i can smell the scent of my choices.
dwelling became too much of a habit.
it was never healthy but i found comfort
in those thoughts. it was okay to go there
i just couldn't stay there.

you remember that time?
when the sky kissed the ocean
and the sunset envied you? well i do.
it happens every full moon. each night.
when i think about you.

no matter how many years pass, i will rewrite
our love. how it began. what you wore. how
we danced… never to compare or exaggerate,
but to always reignite and inspire us to recall
what our love is about.

that is life. isn't it?
relishing moments that take our breath away.

i am clumsy with words
but i fill myself with adjectives
and love-letter phrases
brimmed at capacity
to one day collapse these walls
and water your soul
with words
i've never said

there's something
about you
that heals my sorrow
from just being around you

i lost someone. it was out of my control.
the love of my life vanished and it was like the
world stopped spinning. i felt trapped and
abandoned. the one hope i had was taken
and nothing was quite the same.

you can't fill that hole in my heart.
i don't want you to. we must keep certain wounds
untouched. to remind us that we once really lived.
and some pain you just can't let go of.

parts of me are uneven
and i must accept
that there is beauty
in the unbalanced

there is an old saying:
walk a mile in someone's
shoes to get a glimpse at
what they experience.

i want more than a glimpse.
let me borrow your heart so
that i may feel how it beats.
cradle my ribcage with all
of the stardust in your bones.
transfer to me your sensibility.

set no time or distance limit.
forevermore i want to occupy
all of you. each and every minute.

nothing will break you.
the battles from your past have tested your honor.
strengthened your spirit. sticks and stones may be
cast your way but you block them. you block them.
you will not be broken.

beloved,
you
are
an abyss
of magic

forever is an excuse
an empty unknown
and no matter
how many times i say it
my forevers exist
here and now
in the universe
of just us

i don't have much.
but what i have
i give to you.
love is gold &
baby,
we are rich

i can take hearing
all the no's and
even watch you put
up your defenses.
i will bide my time
and wait. i'll wade
in the deep end of
your smile. because
i know. one day
you'll say yes.
i can stay afloat
'til then.

i've stopped making attempts
to rationalize your actions.
only because my sanity
is too precious. it is not my
place or duty to come up with
a story, when your reason
to leave became an umarked grave.

abandonment with no just cause,
would drive anyone to go mad.

in love,
beggar and king are equal
          - Indian proverb

a partnership has no hierarchy,
     and you and i are one;
     cherish my heart
     as i cherish yours;
     take me as i am,
     make me a better man.

black rum
is what
i call you
love of my life;

you
can drink
with the best
of 'em

cuz
a fountain
full of liquor
doesn't
get drunk
off itself

when i heard what happened,
i felt destroyed. my skin
tightened and the sun turned
deep red: the universe sensed
my anger. i replayed your
misfortune and took it on as if
it was my own wound.
i wanted to wage war, for you.
and i didn't even know you
(when it happened).
but now i do & to know you
is to love you. every part of you.
even the parts i couldn't keep safe.
i know you don't need saving,
you've saved yourself
far too many times,
but i am your warrior lover.
send me into battle.

i am half full but that void in me is a void in you;
even when our fullness propels us to spill into
one another we will always be somewhat empty.

they name tyrannical
storms after you and
tall tales preach
the magnitude of your
grace; you can't help
what people say, you
just go on living. you
snicker at their desire
to build you up
just to tear you down.
they'll never get hold
of the real side
because they're more
interested in the
philosophy of you
rather than the truth
of you.
you are an elusive whisper
in a loud planet.

we took a vow to go out together;
neither of us can bear the thought
of living or loving without the other.

there is love.
there is war.
you can't avoid either.
it's inevitable.
they are no different.
they are two parts
of one process:
when we love,
we love hard &
when we war,
we war hard.

i can lead you to love
but i can't make you jump in.

some dope r&b,
dim red light, vino,
incense & you.
my kind of kush.

my favorite records have scratches across the
surface; hearing cracks in your frequency adds
character to the hypnosis each track puts me
through.

we sleep close
but couldn't be
so far apart.

you can find my love laced
in a 90's melody, full of color.
lights down low. slow jams.
i have a blues for you tonight.
the playlist i made for you
starts out baritone & flares
into soul.

your aura is a collection
of fragmented souls, particles
of all the greats and all the
tragedies. your wanderlust
is mere pilgrimage.
i hope you know
your home is in my heart.

i stayed longer
than i wanted
but if i would have left
a moment sooner
i would have missed you.
so by staying
it worked out.
i almost gave up.
i held onto my convictions
long enough.
was headstrong
long enough. to wait.
i felt the pain.
i felt the agony.
i became the pain.
for love and pain
are no different.

you don't fit in.
it's not that you can't.
you weren't built that way.
your heart is too pure.

you have a southern heart
and a northern temper

we have a classic love.
intricate. simple.

we bump heads and bruise
like anyone else.

we tend to each other's cuts.
no matter how much it hurts.

i too cursed at love
and all it did
was run you further away.

willow trees house
fallen stars
crytallized
in its leaves.
that is how i see you,
darling,
dancing in midair,
magic in the wind.

experience taught you,
hurt raised you.
neither
defined you.

you are a muse.
& in no way
can you change that.

you find
new ways
to love
the same
soul.

i love you.
but you can't keep running away.
stay. and work through this.
i'm stubborn. we both are.
but i can't stand in this fire alone.

hearts don't break.
they beat quietly.
some seek revenge
(a heart for a heart).
you just love harder.
vengeance was in finding happiness.
not in waging war.

you tiptoed.
you shuffled.
you walked the outline of words.
you knew nothing was in them
unless you felt them.

i want to soak up all
the honey off your skin
and drizzle the sugar
on my tongue.

in its purest form, you are raw and sweet;
too little isn't enough, too much i overdose:
regardless of intake, you, darling dear,
enhance my soul.

we will look
back and laugh
at our scars.
not in mockery
or shame but
in praise that
we made it
this far.

we have tried so hard to be different,
love different, think different,
accept different. yet, all of our attempts
fell short.

we have become the same.

if we crash and burn,
we crash and burn.
the rush will be exhilirating
and the flames
will be beautiful.

i loved you way before
i had the courage to tell you.

if all you ever do
is take care of
others who takes
care of you? i am no
savior. just a common
man wanting to exist
in the space between
each breath. to be there
when you think you're 'lone.

i would never
fly my love
half-mast.
it is too sacred.
our elevation is not
of this place and
i can't keep you
a secret. i admit,
at first, i dug a hole
to hide you.
to keep you to myself.
but love is never
to be shackled.

oh, i notice.
i am intuitive to your vibe.
you flee when we get close.
you show up when we drift away.
stay or go.
don't play with my heart.

if you think that
telling you how i feel
is easy, then you can't
claim to know me.
the pressure to keep
things locked up is
what keeps me safe.
i promise to unfold
certain details but
right now i am keeping
my emotions inside.

first heart,
        my only one,
it was dark last night
and the road to you
was narrow
dimly lit.
people didn't wait at crosswalks
they cut corners
diagnally
to wherever, to whomever.
i couldn't get to you quickly
but even when i must leave you
i am always on my way back.
as fast as i can.
just as others travel
to their heartlands.

the love we make
is a spiritual thread
a hand on the chest
a kiss on the forehead
endearing
the sharing of touch
i need it
proves to me
that you're here

i can tell
when you enter
certain spaces.
the air
becomes lighter.
a cool sweet scent
swells inside me.
you are magic
intoxication.

i vow
to pilgrimage
next to you
for as long
as you'll have me.
i am ready
for our forever.

let's sit. close. and in that closeness may we look
for stories we never told one another.

the dictionary shall now replace my pillow.
for each day i wake, my solemn swear to you shall
be to affix new vocabulary best describing all the
letters, numbers, omens that brand your soul.

you are my first and my last breath.
because of you i am full.

i broke my own heart.
pulled it out of my chest.
dug a hole in the garden
behind our house.
planted it like a seed
in the earth.
waiting
for love to sprout.

the worst
parts of you
are why i want
all of you.

what is love? don't give me the cliche rote
definition. i want you to make me feel it. all this
talk is absured misuse. give me something to
plunge into and grip, pinch and be moved by. the
elements you speak of are seasonal. until you offer
me an experience, my heart remains cynical.

you almost left. remember?
your bags were packed. you said goodbye.
the door almost sealed our fate. something
inside me felt fear for the first time.
your tears built a ravine and before they touched
the ground i caught them in my palms. you were
too special. too timeless. it took you almost walking
to the edge to decide what i wanted. i felt you
forever in that moment. it was always you.
remember.

beloved,
i hear you.
i can see why you
think i come and go.
it's no fault of my own.
i'm a wanderer. traveling
between worlds. falling for you
in one and searching for you in the other.

soul to soul. i see
how you stare and
play if off when i
catch you. this tension
is building so get
your feelings out
in the open. what you
wanna say is probably
what i'm thinking.

i can't tell you what you deserve
but go where your smile calls home.

i see that you want to take care of yourself and
face storms in solitude to avoid showing any signs
of misfortune but i'd break my back to lift you up.
every superhuman has their limits, let me fill any
crack that you try to hide to reassure that you are
as powerful as you want to be, and as beautiful as
your vulnerabilities.

trust that i will harbor your tears when you desire
to hold them back.

my memories are made of you.

i thank god for you.
i'll never stop saying that.
there was a shift, a perfect
alignment in our universe that
was written before we met.

love, i can be a wreck and
take it out on you. it is your
sweet laughter that collects
my dark words and kisses them
into light.

i got you. in every sense of my love.
never hesitate to consume my space,
it's yours to occupy.

darling,
my soul smiles no matter
how close or how far you are;
thank you for being
the lover that chose
to love me.

i care for you. more than i care for myself.
and it's hard (so damn hard) witnessing you
go through strain. however, it amazes me
the things you do to push past the pain.

i can't
i can't turn away
i'm in this
in this 'til the last
the last winter
& the winter after that

love—
i believe in it.
even when i don't
understand it.

you heard about me. folks outside my circle filled
you in on third person narratives. something in
your essence told you to listen to your heart and
look into my story. i hope you learned that my
life flirtation is off-beat and old fashioned; i'm a
wanderer with a sage soul.

you teach me
how to
accept the lesson
before, during, and after
a storm.

waiting in the imprint you left behind feels
like miles are between us. yet in that distance
there isn't lonliness—our fiery devotion
keeps me company.

the moment our flirting eyes met,
we became soul tied, connected, one.

the
universe
knows
you
by
name.

your eyes are my gateway drug to paradise;
i teleport (honestly i do) into a calm fog
looking at such an angel.

lover,
that thing you do when you walk towards me,
makes me feel like us two are the only ones.

you are loving music;
every note of you
harmonizes with all of me.

don't sugar coat
the hard stuff.
be bitter. be sour.
be salty. be tart.
my taste buds
can handle it.

the wounds i have carried, you've treated as if they
were your own. together we kneeled and set new
soil—you had every right to turn away and leave
me to face my open graves alone—it hasn't always
been pretty but flowers do grow in trenches when
you pour libations on scars.

i wanna be the one you run to.
let me be the oasis that tucks you in.

wade where i can feel you
my senses will find you

love,
you are
friendly poison
that vined its way
around my heart.

you—the best poem i'll ever know.

i see you
in the leaves
of all shades;
i just hope
that
if a strong wind
gusts you away
the buds that you leave
behind
will blossom

there is no need for me
to hang you on my bedpost
for every web of your soul
is a dreamcatcher
and you caught me
you caught me

in blank stares
i see
dominion
unchartered
kingdom
vacancies
&
one choice
declarations
away
from
reclaiming
dynasty;
i see
mount olympus
in your eyes

i hope i hold you
the way you hold me
like majestic
river nile
bleeding on shore
kissing plants
loving soil
papyrus oil
on skin;
i hope
my tides
do a fraction
of what your
egyptian
perfumed soul
does

you,
my dear,
are the
reason
the land
shifted
and broke off
into
tessellations
and
isolated peninsulas;
your quake
so electric
sends
continents
adrift

i dream of you

with a soft vignette frame

barefoot in the rain

drenched head to heel

with not a care

in the world

even your
shadow
is drenched
in gypsy

they still try to clip your wings
but you'll never fly that low.

you don't follow the main stream,
you go against the current.

drag me into your current
and wash my dirty bones

we live in a world full of subtle glimpses
views into what could be
shimmer like the haze in deserts
it was you
it was you
i finally see the bigger picture
the reflection seemed unreal
it was you
not an optical illusion
it was you
my dream come true

your caramel skin
is a hot fuse detonated by my fingertips.

i have filled my body with too many toxins, too
many love songs, too many fairy tales. along came
a real testimony, and i praise you for blending my
realities with fantasy. you are my wonderland full
of magic.

i love moments like photographing your body
with my lips.

nourish me
feed me
keep me
whole
your light
dipped in
sugar
sweetens
my soul

once. just once.
my only reminder.
don't expect a
reply or a follow up.
no second chance.
once. that will be it.
to see if you
take my heart
for what it's worth
before trying
to weigh it
against
another.

beauty does nothing but be
beautiful. and in your stillness,
beauty doesn't plead for attention.
i love the beauty about you.

you deserved more than what you were given.
the bare minimum was far from enough. it wasn't
me that pulled you away from that desolate island.
the world you carried in your head orbited around
mine that fateful night and it was you that believed
in adventure again. it was you who broke the
shackles of that barren land. i was only the mirror,
a reflective reminder, of the galaxy you needed and
desired.

it won't always feel good
or have strokes of magic.
we will fight
and hold grudges,
even avoid one another.
it will grow old and wrinkled,
might feel like routine.
we will cry.
we will laugh.
we will fear.
it will be unbroken
because we are committed.
we will make it to the end.

our relationship isn't perfect. by any means. but you understand the chaos in my soul. we give each other the space to say, feel, and do things that make us human.

you give me what i need. and force me to own up to my nonsense. our kind of love makes room for mistakes.

you can't expect me to fix us.

you may
have given up
on me
but
it just
made me
love you
even
more

you didn't
disappear
you just
never returned.
i could see you
but you
made me
out to be
nothing
nothing more
than a wind
caught
in your palms;
i was never yours
you were never mine

no matter
how many lovers
you try to fill
that emptiness with
they will fall
into the depths
of your dependence.

return to love
not in someone else
but in yourself.

there's an old saying:
a steady drip of water wears a hole in a rock.

i was that rock. too stubborn to budge. until you
came along and held me in your palms. you weren't
forceful or cruel, you wiped away the built up soot
in my eyes. i did resist. can't pretend otherwise.
but your rain showers were a blessing in disguise.

if you woke up one day
and stopped loving me,
stopped investing in me,
stopped pouring your
everything into us,
stopped loving us,
i would still love you.
you could never stop me
from loving you.
no matter how much
it hurts.

i lost myself
in different worlds.
yet, the world in my
heart needed attention.
it's easier. to escape.
but i need me the most.
to love me. first.

in this boat of solitude i patiently wait. i wait.
i wait. i wait. the dipping sun and far off moon
bleach my sleepless eye; i shan't miss the passing of
that daydream smile. do you notice my movements
and how they mirror every curve and crease your
body dents in my soul? i observe from a distance
yet you occupy all the elements, your everything
surrounds my undeserving stillness. i wait to catch
a glimpse of your face just to throw it right back. i
am not worthy to keep you. i am not worthy to be
but a distant lover for all of eternity.

i count your heartbeats by listening to the air that
escapes your body. when you breathe out i breathe
you in. the energy you release is magic and i long
for my lungs and heart to absorb as much of it.
cover all of me with all of you; you are the oxygen
i need.

water is your energy. love is you. i honor your
phases, cycles, seasons. though at times i may not
see you, you are there in the background, waiting,
hovering. full or half empty, your spirit is with me.
rinse me with your light, child of the night.

set fire to what we have. not to ruin or rapture but to test what our properties are really made of. do we know our boiling point or when our souls start to burn? light us up and take note, we are mad scientists curious to see what chemical reaction unfolds. let us watch our particles dance in flames.

take my heart. take my heart. hold onto it and do,
do what you will. i relinquish all rights and give
power of attorney. take it from me. i bestow it
don't want it. you stole it once but its been yours
since always.

stop. just. stop. stop talking of stars as if they deserve your adoration. stop idolizing unknown darkness and realize that our proximity defies what only astronauts could ever experience.

space is not an exclusive place. we make our own space. we are our own galaxy. when i look to the moon i see you. and the stars are the ones that look down and envy your flame.

faded in the background of my vision i still find your
blurred naked soul beautiful. come close, come
close, sharpen this image. silhouettes mean smoke,
smoke means fire. the dance of your heat breathes
life into me.

i'll never escape my past even though i tried to post
fences around these scars. kevlar isn't even strong
enough to keep them under ground. rather than hide
them i dug up each and every dirty little secret and
poured the bones onto your hands; as the dirt of my
past passed through your fingers some of the poison
leaked into your skin. why did i share my demons
with you? they quake every once in awhile. i guess i
needed to bare my soul releasing me of my sin.

love, hues.

lovehues

COOL RUNNINGS
IN DARK TUNNELS
a novel

BY ADRIAN MICHAEL
COMING SOON

59087341R00089

Made in the USA
Charleston, SC
29 July 2016